# MAKING CONNECTIONS 2:

### An Integrated Approach to Learning English

## Transparency Masters

Carolyn Kessler

Linda Lee

Mary Lou McCloskey

Mary Ellen Quinn

Lydia Stack

Heinle & Heinle Publishers
A Division of Wadsworth, Inc.
Boston, MA 02116, U.S.A.

Manufactured in the United States of America.

ISBN: 0-8384-3837-7

Heinle & Heinle Publishers is a division of Wadsworth, Inc.

10 9 8 7 6 5 4 3 2 1

# Table of Contents

Transparency Master

Page

▲▲▲

## Unit 3 - *Setting Goals*

## Unit 4 - *Making Changes*

▲▲▲

## Unit 5 - *Resolving Conflict*

▲ ▲ ▲

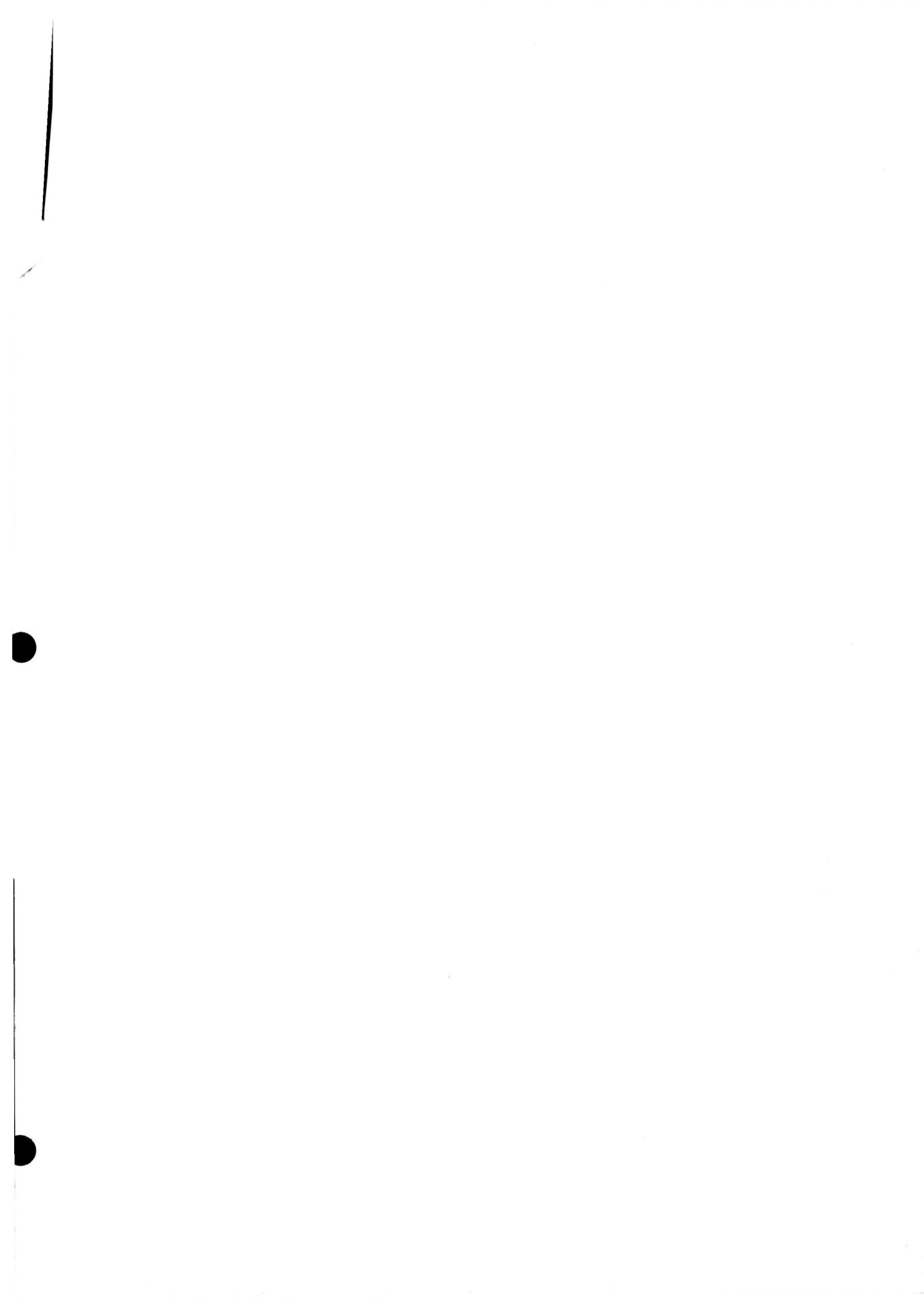